I greatly appreciate you taking the time to read this book. Please consider leaving a review wherever you bought the book or telling your friends about it.

If you would like to learn more about managing your money, sign up to my newsletter at www.lookafteryourpennies.com, follow me on twitter @yourpennies, or Like me on facebook at www.facebook.com/yourpennies.

I am also writing other books for parents and individuals looking for financial freedom and will announce further details via social media and my website.

Copyright © 2014 Fay Arrundale

All rights reserved.

ISBN: 1503316491

ISBN-13: 978-1503316492

Printed by Createspace, an Amazon.com company

Contents

Acknowledgements i

The story behind this book....................................2

Chapter 1...4

Chapter 2...10

The 7 steps 18

Step 1: Have an aim...20

Step 2: Be specific 25

Step 3: Money in, Money out..............................30

Step 4: Where to keep their savings 37

Step 5: How to deal with waning enthusiasm, 'The lull' 45

Step 6: The purchase 52

Step 7: Celebrate, review and repeat...................59

Closing notes: Your role 63

About the author...65

End Notes 67

Acknowledgements

This book could not have been written without the unwavering support of my husband and soul mate, Dave.

This book was written for our children's generation, however I cannot thank our children for their support as our non-stop pre-schooler and our non-sleeping toddler gave very little help.

I would also like to take this opportunity to thank my parents, Mike and Ann Eden, for taking the time to teach me about money and for their constant belief that I would always achieve my dreams, one of which is this book.

The story behind this book

This book was written to support every parent who wants to raise their child to be financially independent but isn't sure where to start.

Having spent seventeen years in the world of banking and corporate life, I developed a growing interest and, some would say, passion for how people manage their money.

In 2011 I joined the realms of parenthood with the birth of my first son who changed my life and introduced me to the world outside the office.

That's when I started to think... What will the world be like when he grows up?

In looking for answers I became scared for a generation growing up in a culture which places huge emphasis on having it all, and having it all NOW.

I wanted to know; who is going to teach my child how to value money and navigate through our evolving virtual money world?

Secondary schools have added financial education to an already packed school curriculum, however according to the Money Advice Service, 'adult financial habits are set by the time a child turns 7'.

Therefore, children must learn how to manage money from a young age and the best people to teach them are their parents.

How can parents, especially those who aren't confident in managing their own money or don't know how to talk about money, teach their children about money?

I decided to start with the idea of teaching your child to save because I feel the ability to save is the foundation for good financial habits.

In writing this book, I had three aims in mind:

1. To give you the confidence to discuss saving money with your children
2. To provide practical steps to apply to everyday life
3. To build financial awareness and independence in your children

That's a whistle-stop tour of how I founded my financial mentoring business 'Look after your pennies'. The name is adapted from the well-known phrase '*Look after the pennies and the pounds will look after themselves*', which was regularly recited by my late father.

My mission is to empower parents to confidently educate their children to become financially independent, whilst learning together how to manage our money in an increasingly virtual world.

For the avoidance of doubt, I am not a financial advisor, I am not working with a financial institution, I won't give advice on financial products and I won't email money-saving tips. What I do is work with children, families, schools and individuals to teach them how to take control of their money.

Chapter 1

I want it now, instant gratification

We are born with an instinct for instant gratification. At birth we cry to ensure our every basic need is met. We demand to be fed when we are hungry, cleaned when we are dirty and cuddled when we want comfort. We need this instinct for survival.

As we grow up we learn that we need to wait for most things. We become good at waiting for our basic needs to be met and most adults have learned to wait for the pleasurable things in life too. We have learned that we can't have everything we want when we want it.

As children, this waiting game can be a difficult lesson to learn.

If you've spent time with a toddler going through this learning journey, you'll have seen that it's one of the biggest challenges for both parents and toddlers. A toddler wants IT now, whether that 'it' is food, a toy, to play or simply just to go in the opposite direction to the one you want them to go in.

Toddlers don't understand why they need to wait; grasping this is part of the transition from a dependent baby to an independent toddler. For parents this is a very trying lesson to teach and most parents will relent to a toddler's demands at some point. But what happens if we give in too much and our children never learn to wait?

Learning patience!

Some children never grasp the need for patience. I certainly know a few adults who are ruled by their overwhelming desire for instant gratification. Sometimes it's for something small, like a coffee or a new pair of shoes, but their impulse for immediate pleasure can result in very poor financial decisions.

An extreme outcome of an adult's lack of self-control can be poor health, addiction problems and an inability to live within their financial means.

Many of the parents I have worked with who have had problems managing their money fall into this category of 'instant gratification'. Whether they gain pleasure from being the first to get new gadgets or the latest season's trends, they often cannot resist spending, despite all rational thought telling them not to.

The problem with spending to fulfill an immediate desire is that often, one desire is replaced with another, leading to a cycle of continuous spending.

Without learning to save it's unlikely that adults with a strong need for instant gratification will have control of their spending and patience to save for longer-term goals.

I believe this need for instant pleasure can be an inbuilt part of our personality, something we are born with; as much a part of our character as kindness, for example.

So, what has any of this got to do with helping your child learn to save? I believe that having a greater understanding of both our inbuilt need for instant gratification[i] and some people's natural disposition towards it, can allow us to adapt how we can help our children learn to wait.

Is your child a 'Craver' or a 'Saver'?

Most children will learn patience (to some degree) and how to manage their frustrations over not getting what they want immediately. I believe that the extent to which we learn to control our frustrations has a direct link to how we handle other aspects of our lives, including how we deal with money.

When thinking about instant gratification, I believe there are two types of money personality; a 'Craver' and a 'Saver'. For me, these are on a scale, from slightly one more than the other to a 'definitely that one'.

Some of us are born as Cravers, always seeking instant gratification. Once we have what we craved, we move on to the next thing. We all know someone who desperately wants a top of the range car, or a luxurious holiday or to wear the latest fashion.

Cravers tend to be risk takers, they are likely to try out new technologies, they are curious and determined, and they want to be the first to find out about new products or services.

Cravers gain their pleasure from exploring new things and as such can get bored quickly, always looking for what they can explore next.

At the other end of the scale, Savers are likely to be more reserved, cautious in decision-making, part of the crowd. They might wait to see other people trying new things before taking the leap themselves.

Savers gain pleasure from security. After much contemplation over whether to buy something, a Saver will get a lot of pleasure from that single purchase. A Saver is likely to have a purse full of coupons and loyalty cards, however this can mean they are enticed to compromise because an alternative option is cheaper (but not necessarily as good).

From my observations, I believe we are largely born with these traits; we are either naturally Cravers or Savers, to differing degrees.

We all know the sibling who eats all of their Christmas chocolates before Boxing Day is over, and the sibling who savours theirs, and still has some left by Easter.

However, I also believe that the way in which our parents handle our demands in our early years has a huge impact on the extent to which these traits dictate our lives.

Do you recognise yourself in either of the two personality types? If you do, how do you think your type impacts the way you manage money? Do you think this has an impact on your child?

Consider your child, which type do you think they naturally edge towards?

So, does this matter?

I believe this natural preference towards Craving or Saving is important because it plays a role in lots of aspects of a child's life, including their ability to learn and their ability to share.

Cravers find it particularly difficult to hold back and wait for things in life. Parents of Cravers have said to me, '*My child wants everything now and won't stop nagging until they have got it, then within a day they have moved on to the next thing that they want. How do I teach them to wait?*'

The honest answer is you can't change their personality, however you can teach your child to develop self-discipline and encourage them to see the value in what they have.

With Cravers you can help them decide on the one thing they want the most, rather than feeling the need to have it all. You can help them to prioritise and think a bit more about why they want something.

Cravers can be impulsive in their decision-making and easily influenced by others. The best approach for helping Cravers is to ask them questions before they make a decision and to encourage them to reflect on their choices.

Savers are much less likely to want to spend and may even deprive themselves of joining in and not allow themselves to have things they want.

Savers may also hold on to things for a special occasion, when the reality is the thing they are saving goes out of date and is no longer wanted by the time they allow themselves to use it.

Savers are likely to be indecisive and overwhelmed if they have too many options. Helping a Saver filter out information in order to focus on what is important to them can help them make financial decisions more easily, reducing their anxiety.

It doesn't matter which type your child is, neither one is better than the other, but what does matter is how you help your child gain a balanced perspective.

Both types bring challenges to how your child manages money.

Regardless of their personality type, there are many things in life that we simply cannot have instantly. This is especially true of money. The reality is that very few of us have an abundance of money to spend on whatever we want.

Chapter 2

Seeing the world through your child's eyes

I started to think about how, as parents, we are the single most influential factor in our children's lives.

Just listen to a toddler talk, often they can sound just like their mum or dad, they say phrases far beyond their comprehension, they use facial expressions they are mimicking but don't understand, they are absorbing everything we, as parents, do.

Money is no exception to this; our children are watching us spend, hearing our discussions and consuming the things that we buy.

However, as much as we want to shape their attitudes and values, the reality is the world they are growing up in looks very different to the one we knew as children. They are also far more exposed to other influences outside of our control.

The following list is by no means exhaustive, but gives an indication of the changing world our children live in:

- Availability of television 24 hours a day from multiple channels (most of which have commercials)
- Endorsement or sponsorship of products and services, particularly aimed directly at children
- Increased use of technology; computers, mobile phones and tablets. 3.5 million children under the age of 8 have a tablet[ii] (such as an iPad), with parents spending £5.6 billion a year on gadgets for their children
- Women are having children at an older age. Parents are likely to have had a career and possibly greater disposable income before having

children
- Increased cost of living and expectation that both parents work
- Wealthier grandparents who are less likely to live close to their grandchildren
- Less conventional families – single parents, step and half siblings, multi-generation living
- Expectation to attend multiple activities, entertainment and after-school clubs

With so much change, the world can seem a daunting place to us, let alone to our children.

How can we protect their childhood and at the same time prepare them to become financially independent?

This chapter focuses on how much our world is changing and, although we will continue to be a significant influence on our children, how we can support them (while learning ourselves) as they navigate through this brave new world.

The future of money

In the 17 years I have worked in banking, the way in which we manage and spend our money has changed beyond recognition.

I believe there are three main trends, which will change the future of how we manage money.

1. The way we pay for things

We are using cash less and less in favour of cards, with 91% of the UK adult population having a debit card and 61% owning a credit card[iii].

Ever wondered why you receive so many invitations to get a new credit card? It's because of our love of card payments. The UK now accounts for an astonishing 73% of the European credit card market, with 75% of all spending in retail stores being carried out by cards rather than cash.

Our cards are able to do more than ever before. Along with getting cash from a cash machine and paying for items in store, we use them to pay for things we order online, pay for goods and services using contactless[iv] technology, capture loyalty points and even as a ticket for the London Underground.

Technology is moving so quickly, it won't be long before we are paying by tapping our mobile phones or watches against a payment machine.

Many of our purchases are now made when we're not even present, compare this to a largely cash society less than 50 years ago.

2. Where we save or borrow our money

As consumers, we have lost confidence in the established banks and are instead choosing to open accounts with the supermarkets (e.g. Tesco Bank) or established brands (e.g. Marks & Spencer Money).

To adapt to our increase in online spending, companies such as Paypal have introduced yet another way to pay.

We are finding new ways to borrow or invest; not happy with the returns or service we have received from the established banks, we are opting to join Credit Unions or invest in property.

A controversial addition to the UK banking market is the payday loan. Companies lend small amounts (typically less than £250) for a short period (less than two weeks).

Payday loans should be used only for emergencies due to their very high interest repayments. Despite recent changes to regulation[v] to limit the amount of interest a payday lender can charge, they can still charge up to twice as much as the amount borrowed, if you borrow £100 you could repay £200.

3. The way we manage money

The monthly printed bank statement delivered through the post is virtually archaic.

We use our mobile phones to transfer money and check balances; visits to our local branch are no longer essential for everyday banking.

We have multiple places we keep or borrow our money from, no longer are all our funds with one trusted bank, as it might have been for our parents. We now chase better rates and move money frequently.

We have more accounts to keep track of.

We use far more ways to keep our money; safe from PIN's on cards, to passwords, little devices we put our cards in to generate secure codes. Long gone are the days where our signature was our moneys security.

My point to all this is gone are the days when you only had to manage physical money. When you had £40 in your purse to last until payday, you knew you really could only spend what you had and it was easy to track how much you had left – you simply opened your purse.

Our children will need to learn to manage their money in a virtual world.

As parents we need to learn with them. How will we continue to look after our pennies when we never physically have any?

Brave new world

Let's paint a picture of how the future might look for our children in 10 years' time:

- Employment is likely to move towards multiple jobs, freelancing and self employment
- Changes in employment will lead to irregular income patterns, a monthly salary from one employer is likely to be the exception, not the norm
- We will be spending more money on services which we didn't even have 30 years ago – broadband, downloading services (films, books, music, games), technology – in particular mobile phones
- Continued growth of convenience foods
- Greater emphasis on looking after our personal data, particularly online
- Cash will be slowly replaced with virtual payment methods

This is not a gloomy picture; these are changes impacting the world we live in. We need to work out how we can help our children develop good financial habits in this ever-changing environment where we are probably learning with them.

How will they learn to survive in this new world?

After years of campaigning by a number of charities and businesses, from September 2014 secondary school pupils (aged 11 to 16) in the UK have Financial Education in their curriculum, covering topics such as debt, income tax and money management.

This is a significant step forward and fantastic for our 11+ children. It is likely to cover money in a different way to that of parents, focusing on the practical side of money management.

Will this new curriculum teach them everything you want them to know about money? No. Should we give schools sole responsibility to teach our children about money? No.

Alongside formal teaching there are the "softer" aspects of money management, such as how money makes us feel and how we place a value on things we want and need. I believe these lessons are best learned from within a family as they essentially link to your family's values.

Expecting secondary schools to educate our children on money is too late, 'adult financial habits are set by the time a child turns 7' (according to the Money Advice Service). By the age of 11 they will have very strong views and spending habits, which may be difficult to change.

I am a strong believer that we learn best by doing; there is no substitute for experience. Having physical cash in their hands, in a shop and deciding to buy something is an experience that will give our children both the satisfaction of making a purchase and the disappointment when they can't have something. These feelings have much more impact on their ability to manage their money than understanding the difference between a current account and a credit card.

Parents and families need to take the lead in showing their children how to take control of their own finances.

Schools will compliment and support us, but ultimately we need to take responsibility in the same way as we teach our children to dress themselves and cross the road.

Be aware of constant temptation

Point out to children from a young age that we are bombarded with opportunities to eat, play and spend. Our children face far more temptation and are exposed to more sophisticated and targeted marketing now than at any other time.

Studies[vi] have shown that until they are eight, most children cannot differentiate between a sales pitch and a story. As parents, it's our responsibility to make our children aware of the ways products are sold to us.

My concern with child-targeted marketing is that it often uses endorsements from children's television characters; encouraging children to want food, drinks and toys we might not want them to have. It's classic marketing, we can't avoid it and individually we can't change it, but we can make our children aware of what it is they are getting.

As our children get older we can try to teach them the value of what they are buying. Ask your child to consider what the endorsed product actually is when the packaging is removed and whether it's still worth it.

> **Tip**: Limit the exposure your children have to marketing aimed at them – monitor their web use, turn off pop-up boxes, check mobile phone apps, record programmes on television so that you can forward over the adverts, be aware of the type of magazines and other literature they have access.

Try to increase your own awareness of how you are influenced by marketing and brands. When shopping, particularly food shopping, it's very easy amid a huge array of choice to opt for the endorsed product or brand.

Consider the things you say when your children are around, especially when your child asks for something. Try to give the reason behind your decision to say 'no'; for example, 'We're not going to buy that, because we would prefer to spend our money going to the cinema'.

A Craver is more likely to find the allure of marketing harder to resist and is likely to be drawn to every temptation. If this is the case its even more important to limit the amount of marketing they are exposed to.

Savers are likely to find the bombardment of marketing overwhelming, giving them too many options and things to think about before making a decision. If this is the case, help them to prioritise what they want before venturing out to the shops.

The 7 steps

How will this guide help you?

Given how important I feel a financial education is, and that I believe an introduction to managing money starts at home, I have put together this 7-step guide to support parents and explain savings in a way that is simple but effective.

This guide has been written for anyone who plays a significant role in a child's life, including parents, guardians, grandparents, aunts, uncles and teachers.

I hope that it helps you feel more confident about talking to your child about money; I would be ecstatic if it also helps you feel more confident about managing your own money.

How to use this book

Given the time pressures faced by most parents, this book has been written to be read step by step or to dip in and out of sections as you need to.

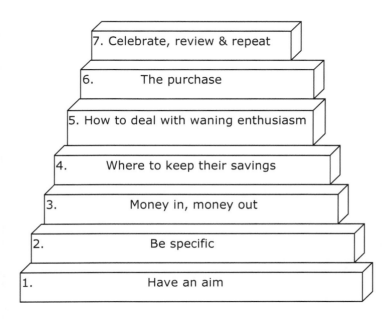

Step 1: Have an aim

Knowing what we are aiming for makes us much more likely to achieve it. Whether our aim is to buy a house, move jobs or lose weight, all require us to identify what it is we want and to set ourselves a target.

Why have a goal?

As adults, we are far more motivated and focused if we have a goal. This is the same for children.

Take a moment to think about most children's activities; learning to swim, Brownies and Cubs, martial arts, learning to play a musical instrument; they all have a way to recognise your child's achievements and have clear steps to progress – grades in music, distance in swimming, belts in martial arts.

These 'systems' of progression towards a bigger goal, for example, playing the piano well or swimming unaided, use exactly the same principles;

1. Clear and transparent steps (grades/stages)
2. Sense of achievement on reaching them
3. Clear end goal and visual reward (certificate, sew-on badge, belt)

These principles are particularly useful for children who respond well to structure and help encourage self-discipline.

Having targets set by others is useful, but when it comes to money, it's really helpful if we can teach our children how to set their own goals.

We can be reluctant to introduce children to money at a young age, feeling we need to protect them from the harsh realities of life, however of all the lessons our children learn (musical instruments, sports, arts) you can guarantee that money management is the one skill they will still be using in 20 years' time.

Deciding on their own goal

The first piece of advice I give to parents is that you need to allow your children to set their own goals, you cannot choose for them. Well, you can but the chances are they won't be motivated to achieve them.

By all means make suggestions on the types of things they might like to save for, but ultimately they need to decide exactly what they want. As a result of making their own decision children are learning that to set an aim they have to compromise and prioritise their own wants.

The setting of a goal can be difficult for Cravers and Savers in different ways. Cravers are likely to find it harder to compromise and stick with one thing. Cravers are likely to lose motivation more quickly if they change their minds about their goal. By their nature, Cravers like new and shiny things and are likely to be easily distracted.

Savers may struggle to decide that any option is good enough. Savers are more likely to talk themselves out of each goal; always waiting for a better option, and because of this Savers may appear to be indecisive.

> *Tip:* Encourage children to set their own goals; ownership of what they are aiming for is a big part of the feeling of success.

How to help them choose their goal

So, how do you help children think about what they want? Which means not what their friends have, not what they have seen advertised and not because their favourite character is on the packaging.

For younger children (aged 10 and under), the way to help them decide what they want is to take an interest in what they are enjoying at the moment. What's a long-standing favourite that never quite makes it into the charity bag? When you go away for the weekend, what item do they take with them?

Once you have spent a bit of time watching where they get their enjoyment, start to look for a pattern, for example:

- Things they can role play with
- Things to make or build
- Puzzles, things that need solutions
- Social, play together toys like board games

This can also be things they would like to do, rather than material objects, such as a trip to the bowling alley, cinema, farm or soft play.

> **Tip:** Finding something children are motivated to save for is like finding a sport or musical instrument to play; it's likely to take a few attempts to find the one they fall in love with. The motivation to save comes from finding 'the One'.

Older children (10 years and above) are more likely to know what it is they want. An older child's problem is likely to be learning to compromise and choosing just one thing to save for.

If your child is struggling to think of a goal, ask yourself the following questions to help think of ideas:

- Are they excited when they talk about what they have been playing?
- Do they treat the item as if it were a prize antique? (Possibly taking it to bed for safe keeping from younger siblings, my son regularly sleeps with his favourite cars.)
- Are they collecting something for which there is a next edition?
- Do they mention it to other people, such as grandparents?

Once you think they've found the 'One', have a celebratory moment, that's half the challenge.

You don't need to like their choice!

We have all seen instances of a child wanting something that a parent doesn't want them to have; another Barbie in a different dress, yet another Lego set or simply something plastic with their favourite character on the front.

Speaking from experience of buying presents for nieces and nephews, if you're not in the 'zone' for that item, it's like buying something from another planet. I still can't say for sure that I understand Moshi Monsters or Skylander, or could tell each character apart, let alone pronounce their names, but it gives the children huge amounts of pleasure to receive something they are genuinely interested in, even if I'm not.

As much as you can help to guide them in their decision – *'You've already got one like that'*, *'It's not good value for money'* and *'You're paying for the brand'* – remember this is *their* goal, it's their 'dream' to achieve.

At this point think about the long-term aim of teaching them to save, even if you really don't want them to bring home more of what they already have.

Step 2: Be specific

Like most goals we set for ourselves, if we're not specific about what we're trying to achieve we are likely to lose interest as we're not sure what we're aiming for.

Being vague about a goal is like setting off on a journey and not knowing your end destination.

Deciding on a goal can be easy; being specific about it will bring it to life.

If you've ever worked in a large business you will probably have had personal objectives for your job, and if so those objectives probably had to adhere to rules on how to set a goal. The two most popular models use acronyms (well this is in business land), these are S.M.A.R.T. and G.R.O.W.

As mocking as I was of these acronyms when I had to use them in my professional life, I hate to admit it but they can be really useful.

Let me briefly explain each one and see if they might work for you and your child.

S.M.A.R.T

This stands for:

S	Specific
M	Measurable
A	Achievable
R	Relevant
T	Time bound

This model is widely used when thinking of the detail of goal setting. The steps are fairly self-explanatory, however I have added some of my thoughts after using them for nearly 20 years.

Specific – the exact detail of what it is you are trying to achieve. For a child this could be the model type, the exact book title, the exact version of an X box game or app.

The reason I like Specific is because it's clear to all what it is they want, with no ambiguity.

Measurable – allows you to see where you are now and helps plan the route to where you want to get. For savings, Measurable is likely to be a monetary value and time.

Achievable – we can often fail to reach a goal simply because the goal we set for ourselves was out of reach before we started.

Expecting our children to save for their own bike costing £79 when they receive a pound a week of pocket money is unrealistic. Even the most extreme Saver will struggle to save for over a year for one item. Make sure that the target they have in their sights is sensible.

> ***Tip:*** *Are there any factors outside of their control which may prevent them from achieving their goal – can you foresee these?*

Relevant – this suggests the goal needs to be appropriate, saving for a goal they cannot achieve, for example, a DVD for 18-year-olds. Relevant also means it needs to be significantly important enough for the child to be motivated to save for.

Time bound – this is important for a child, as their definition of time can feel somewhat different to ours. Expecting a 5-year-old to save for more than a couple of weeks and remain focused is asking a lot, as they may not only lose interest but also become frustrated.

A 10-year-old is much more likely to save for a couple of months if what they have set in their sights is something they are truly motivated to save for and they can see their progression towards it.

In my opinion, setting a target date is one of the most important parts of goal setting, it allows you to visualise when you have reached your goal. A date makes it more real.

For younger children who haven't yet grasped time (weeks and months), you could put a chart on the wall for them to cross off each day or week.

G.R.O.W

The G.R.O.W model is used in business for both goal setting and problem solving. Some of the letters in the acronym have different versions.

G	Goal
R	Reality
O	Obstacles (Options)
W	Will (Way forward)

I have had more success using this model with older children (10 years old +), as it requires a different level of understanding of the goal. In particular, considering obstacles that might get in their way, for example, getting side tracked and spending their savings on a trip to the cinema with friends.

'Goal' and 'Reality' are essentially asking 'What are they aiming for?' and 'Is it possible to reach?'

I particularly like 'Option', when discussing money. Helping children realise they have a choice and there are options. Exploring how they can best spend £10, whether it's buying one larger item, lots of smaller regular purchases, saving a bit and spending a bit or even buying for someone else.

Being aware there are options gives a sense of ownership as they get to decide which option they choose.

Understanding you are in control of how you spend your money (as a child at least, it gets a bit more complicated for adults – you can't choose not to pay for food), is absolutely key to building sound financial decision-making.

Finally, 'Will' or 'Way Forward' is great to consider because it assumes you've set your goal, fantastic, now what do you do with it? Where do you go from here?

For me, 'Will' is about compromise and motivation. Can they forfeit treats for their goal? This step is particularly difficult for Cravers, who set out with good intentions but may find it hard to stick to them.

Milestones

Another aspect of being specific is setting milestones, points (often time or money goals) when you can pause and celebrate how far they've come, a little bit like the structures in their activities, such as achieving swimming badges.

The more engaged your child is in defining the goal and working out how they are going to meet it, the more likely they are to be committed to sticking to it.

> *Tip:* These goal-setting techniques are applicable in many parts of learning and preparing for adult life, from homework to planning a birthday party. They are not just a basis for saving money.

Step 3: Money in, Money out

So the goal is set, you both know how much is needed to achieve their aim; it's time to talk money.

Why do we have money?

For younger children you may need to start by explaining why we have money. In its simplest form we are teaching them we can give something we have of value and exchange it for something we want. This could be that they swap one of their own toys for a friend's toy.

When a child understands that we can swap things we have for things we want, they can then begin to learn that we can also use money to do this.

It's at this point I would introduce them to the basics of currency, such as the denominations of coins – 1p, 2p, 5p, 10p etc. I have found younger children are more engaged when you use physical or visual stimulus, for example pretend money and shop tills are a great way to introduce the idea of exchanging money to buy something.

Younger children are unlikely to distinguish between the different amounts of money and are likely to believe that a 10p coin is more valuable than a £1 coin because it's bigger. It will take time for them to understand the differences, particularly under 5s who are unlikely to be able to count to 100.

It isn't a big concern if they get confused over the coins, the key is that they understand that the things they want have a value in the form of a price.

Older children will have a greater awareness of how much things cost and may have started to compare the values of different items. With £5 they could buy a magazine and sweets, or they could buy a DVD.

The challenge with older children is grasping how much money we have available, especially with the use of payment cards (debit/credit cards), as they never really see how much is being spent in total or where the money is coming from.

How do we get money?

Teach children we are given money in exchange for something we do, which we call work. Whether you fix cars, make people feel better, cook for others or sell things, explain to your child what you do and that you are given money to do it.

The money that you earn is then used to buy the things that your family needs and wants.

For older children you can explain how we spend money on the things we need, like paying our mortgage or rent, electricity bills, buying food, paying for our cars. This probably won't be the slightest bit interesting to them, but they need to learn that some of our money has to be spent on essentials before we can spend money on the things that we want.

Your child's source of money is most likely to be you, their parents, and possibly grandparents. However, I am in favour of children learning that money is an exchange and not just given. Therefore making pocket money conditional on things you expect of them, like good behaviour, putting their clothes in the washing basket and making their bed, is good practise for the real world.

I also firmly believe that children value the money they have when they have had to earn it. They will think harder before spending a pound they have earned clearing up leaves in the garden than they will before spending a pound that has been given to them.

The most important thing to learn about the money coming in is, that sadly, there isn't an endless supply. Teaching our children that we have a limited amount of money and we need to decide how we spend it is fundamental to their understanding of managing their money.

Their money in and money out

Sit with your child to work out their 'earnings'. What money do they have coming in – pocket money, money for chores around the house, money from grandparents, birthday money or money they have already saved. This is their starting point.

Then look at their 'outgoings'. What do they spend their money on each week – sweets, mobile phone, downloading apps, cinema and sticker collections etc.

If your child is old enough and computer savvy, the best way to record their money is on a spreadsheet, but a piece of paper will do the job just as well.

For younger children you can use play money or small coins to show the money they have and the money they spend.

Below is a very basic example of what your child's money in/money out could look like:

	Weekly Money in	Weekly Money out
Pocket money from parents	£5.00	
Washing Granddads car	£1.50	
Weekend sweets		£1.25
Sticker collection		£1.00
School tuck shop (30p per day)		£1.50
Mobile phone app game		£1.50
Total	**£6.50**	**£5.25**
Remaining each week	£1.25	

Based on the above example, it will take a child eight weeks to save £10 (£10 divided by £1.25).

Budgeting!

Once your child understands how to note down the money they get in and the money they spend, they have the basic steps of that scary thing called budgeting.

Most adults don't have a budget. There are a number of reasons for this; we lack confidence in using numbers, we feel we don't have the time to work it out, there is always something more exciting to do or we prefer not to know.

I can't emphasise enough how important awareness is. Many adults would be in a better financial position if they knew what they were spending their money on and then decided to adapt their habits.

If your child is aware of how much they have and what they spend it on, they are in a strong position to be in control of their money.

> **Tip:** I'll let you into a secret; controlling the money you have going out is far easier that getting more money in. As simple as that sounds, still as adults we don't control what we have going out and spend far too much time chasing 'new' money or thinking that we need to earn more rather than considering how we are spending.

Having a budget allows your child to decide how they are going to spend future money. Having something specific to save for will allow your child to 'play' with their budget and possibly change how they spend their future money.

Using the above example, if your child wants to buy the item in four weeks, instead of eight, they will need to save on average £2.50 per week (£10 divided by 4 weeks=£2.50), an extra £1.25 in addition to the £1.25 they already save.

Since they have a budget, they can see that if they gave up their weekend sweets then they would achieve their savings goal in four weeks rather than eight. Alternatively, they could reduce the amount they spend on the tuck shop to 50p (saving £1) and reduce the amount they spend on their mobile phone game by 25p.

The same applies to their money in. Earning extra money by doing jobs around the house; perhaps gardening at Gran's house, walking the dog etc, will reduce the time it takes them to save the money they need.

There are a number of mobile phone apps which play on this idea of learning how to budget and the exchange of value, the ones I am familiar with are Moneyville and NatWest Bank's Pigby's Fair. However, there are many similar games aimed at children.

Tip: Budgets are there to be used and explored. Let your child see what happens when they take different actions and the consequences of those actions.

Is it wrong to give money in place of birthday or Christmas presents?

Prior to having children I thought giving money as a gift was a lazy option – '*I don't know what to buy them, so I'll give them money*'.

However, since having children and realising how overwhelming mountains of presents can be, my opinion has changed. While it's lovely to receive a present, it can also be a waste if it's not something they want or will use.

I have slowly come to the conclusion that as children get older, money is a more and more favoured gift. If money is given as a present, I offer the following advice:

- Be sensible with the amount of money given directly to the child; £10 or £20, any more should go into a savings account
- If you don't want to give cash, consider a gift card (replacing paper gift vouchers). Gift cards are well received by teenagers as they give them an independent way to shop.
- Gift cards are also a good way of contributing to something you know they are saving for by purchasing from the retailer they will spend at. You can also buy gift vouchers/certificates to spend online. Most retailers have gift cards
- A small gift to unwrap, particularly a personalised gift, can be nice to receive, as getting everything they asked for doesn't leave room for surprises
- Make sure the child's parents know you have handed out money so that it's not lost in the card envelope
- A thank you card stating how the money was spent is polite and lets the person know how the money was spent

Step 4: Where to keep their savings

When your child has decided what they are saving for and committed to start saving, the next step is deciding where the money will be kept.

I'm quite old fashioned in that I like a moneybox. I like the physical presence of money and being able to see the funds growing as I save, and when I'm tempted to spend I imagine the jar empty and all that hard work without the reward of what I am saving for.

However, I am realistic enough to recognise that I am prehistoric in my love of physical money. I know our children are growing up in a world of virtual money.

For younger children (10 years and under)

I have found that younger children respond well to physical cash, it feels more real than an online account. I would advocate using a moneybox where they can see their funds growing each week.

I have also found that younger children are excited by adding coins to their collection, which is great if you want to use small denominations, so that even a simple task around the house can be rewarded with 10p.

In America, when teaching children about money it is very common to use three jars/moneyboxes. These are based on one for spending, one for saving and one for sharing (charity).

I really like the idea of 'jam-jarring' (having different pots for different purposes) and think it works well for children to separate out their money. Mentally they treat each jar differently, they are less likely to dip into the savings jar when the spending jar is empty, when compared to how a child might treat their money if all of it is in the same jar.

Decorating the jar or moneybox is also a good way of remembering what they are saving for. A picture or drawing of what they are saving for continues this feeling of ownership.

The reason a glass jam jar works so well is because you can see clearly what's inside, so there is a visual reminder of the amount saved.

Even a ceremonial counting of the money every few weeks will help to keep their motivation high (and help their understanding of different coin sizes and values).

The key is working out what it is that will motivate and bring pleasure to your child. The novelty of a jam jar and the physical act of putting money in each week might bring its own enthusiasm.

Younger children are less likely to be saving significant amounts, therefore security is not as much of a problem as for older children.

For younger children who would like a virtual account, you can use a number of mobile phone apps or websites such as Moneyville or NatWest's Pigby's Fair, which are virtual towns where your child can earn and spend silver and gold coins and learn how to manage virtual money.

For older children (10 years and above)

For older children or larger sums of money it's worth considering opening a bank or savings account, for safety and to teach children about the benefits of interest.

I consider there to be two types of accounts for children, the first is what I call a virtual piggy bank, and the second is the more traditional savings or current accounts.

Before continuing, I would like to emphasise I am not a financial advisor and I am not directly making recommendations of the accounts I mention, I just want to make you aware of the type of accounts available so that you can consider which might work for you and your child.

Virtual piggy banks

The virtual piggy bank accounts are relatively new and are often run by charities or non-banking organisations. These accounts commonly offer two accounts, one for the parent and one for the child, these accounts are linked and the parent retains overall control of setting limits.

These types of accounts generally don't earn interest and may charge a fee.

I've listed three of the better known ones in a table with a comparison of their features and benefits[vii]:

Table 1: Virtual piggy banks

	GoHenry	Roosterbank	Qwiddle
Purpose	Replicates a junior current account, automatic payment of pocket money	Online piggy bank, focused on savings rather than day to day money management	Structured reward account. All money stored online
Target age	8-18 year olds	Not specified	Not specified
Payment Card (ATM)	Yes, prepaid Visa debit	No	No, use of Paypal for payments
Fees	£1.97 per child per month	None for basic, can upgrade to Premium £20.99 per year	None
Other features and benefits	Ability to set spending rules.

Money can be transferred back from the child. | Ability to set savings targets | Set goals, add chores for monetary rewards.

Educational based |

Virtual piggy banks are useful for children who are too old for moneybox style savings and too young for a current account or savings account. They neatly introduce children to the concept of tracking and earning money in a safe environment.

Traditional savings and current accounts

Most banks and building societies offer accounts for children but before heading to your local branch, it's worth considering what features and benefits you want from the account.

Let's start with savings accounts; there are two types of savings accounts for children's money:

1. A long-term savings account: purpose of saving larger sums of money for when the child reaches 18 years of age to contribute towards a larger expense such as a car, house deposit or university. Parents and grandparents often both contribute. These can be Junior ISAs[viii], Premium Bonds[ix] or other forms of investment. The advantages of these accounts are they often have better rates of interest and can be tax-free savings (by not paying tax on the interest you get to keep more of the interest earned).

2. A regular savings account: purpose of adding smaller sums regularly, money can be taken out when needed. Great for adding larger amounts such as birthday and Christmas money. Often operated at the branch for paying in and withdrawing money. The child is likely to have more control over this type of account, but legally before the age of 7 they will not be able to access the money without you.

When trying to explain interest payments to a child, I describe it in the following way: *'when you put your money in a bank, you're lending them your money, so they pay you'*. The money they pay you is called interest.

If asked what the bank does with their money or why they pay interest, I would answer in the simplest way: '*the banks lend the money to someone else who needs it and charges that person for borrowing, they then have money they can give to you as interest*'.

When explaining how interest is worked out, I use a simple example such as; If the interest rate is 10%, the bank pay you 10p a year for every £1 you save.

Once happy with the concept of interest, you could explain the added bonus of compound interest. This is where you earn interest on the interest the bank has already paid you, which means your savings grow faster.

Using the earlier example, compound interest would mean your 10p interest a year would become 11p the following year because your savings are £1.10 (initial £1 plus your first years 10p interest).

The higher the interest rate and the longer you keep the money in the bank the more interest you are paid.

The decision on type of savings account depends on whether you want the account to be somewhere you save for your children or whether it's an account you want them to control.

Current accounts for children are very similar to those we use as adults, with the exception of no overdraft facility (an overdraft is classed as borrowing, you need to be at least 18 years of age before you can legally borrow money).

Most children's current accounts can be opened from 11 to 18 years of age, after 18 they can apply for a standard current account.

Choosing an account can be difficult, however there are a lot of money comparison websites where you can search and compare suitable accounts.

Parents normally have to go into a branch to open accounts for a child, taking their birth certificate, with the parent or guardian acting as a signatory.

When looking at current accounts for children, consider features such as:

- Do you want them to have their own debit card? (Under the age of 16 years old the financial institution needs to have your permission to provide a debit card)
- How do you want them to manage their money? Mobile phone apps, online banking, paper statements?
- How do you want them to pay money in? Automatic transfers from your account for their pocket money?
- Does the account pay any interest? If so, is there a minimum balance?
- How much control do you want to have over the money?
- Additional features such as managing their money with text alerts

When deciding whether a savings account or a current account is most appropriate, ask yourself which is more important; that the money saved earns interest (long term savings account) or that your child learns how to manage their money (regular savings or current account)?

There are no rules to say your child should have only one type of account, they can jam-jar their money using a mixture of savings and current accounts.

> **Tip:** The most important thing is finding out what works for them and what you, as their parent, are comfortable with.

Measuring – make it visual

Regardless of where the savings are kept, having a way to measure how they are doing will add some fun and keep their aim alive, think church roof appeal fund.

You could draw a chart on a piece of paper or on Photoshop with a picture of their aim at the top and milestones clearly marked. This represents how they are going to reach their reward.

Younger children in particular respond well to this type of reward chart.

> **Tip:** Make the milestones in smaller increments so that they can see they are working towards their goal quite easily. For example, £1 increments or 5% of the value of what they are saving for. It will also feel good to be able to mark off the progress more frequently.

Choose a way to mark off reaching each milestone – colouring it in, using a highlighter pen, stickers or painting. It might be worth making it removable on the off chance they dig in to their savings and the 'pot' reduces! (Very likely for a Craver personality).

Once completed, put the finished chart somewhere they can regularly see it as a reminder of their goal; on the kitchen wall, the fridge door or their bedroom door.

Step 5: How to deal with waning enthusiasm, 'The lull'

A child's enthusiasm is no different to an adult's in that it starts off high, full of optimism, then dips over time, then increases as the goal gets closer. The difference with adults is we've learned to work through the lull using different tactics.

This can be the most difficult step and regardless of how enthusiastic a child might have been at the beginning, two weeks in they may forget why they started saving in the first place.

Following a plan can take patience, resilience, optimism and willpower. Lessons that take children a while to learn. A plan to save is no exception.

> *Tip:* By learning about the lull, they are experiencing exactly the emotions and feelings they will experience when saving for their first car, a gap year or even a house.

Finding ways to get through the lull takes plenty of practise, they won't learn it all from their first attempt at saving.

By helping our children experience what it feels like to go through this stage in a safe environment, we are allowing them to feel frustrated, angry and disheartened at not having got what they want yet. We are also supporting them as they find solutions and manage their emotions. This experience is relevant to all aspects of their lives, not just managing money.

If we know their enthusiasm is likely to dip at some point during the saving journey, how can we support them?

5 ways to keep the goal alive

There are a number of ways you can encourage them to keep going, these are my top five:

1. Keep it real

Part of the reason that children (and adults) lose interest in reaching a goal is because it stops feeling real, it feels like it's never going to be reached.

So bring it back to the front of their minds; put reminders everywhere, put pictures of the thing they are saving for on the kitchen notice board, on their toy box or school bag.

Talk to them about what they will do when they have it, how they might feel.

Read reviews online about the item, make them start to feel it's within their grasp.

Whether it's new trainers, toys or a Playstation game, remind them what they are saving for and how they will feel when they have reached their goal.

2. Regular praise and encouragement

Never underestimate how much your regular encouragement will spur a child on in those final few days and weeks of saving.

I am not suggesting all-out gushing of how brilliant they are, but the odd comment on how proud you are of them and how well they have done will make a huge difference.

Mention it to grandparents, aunts and uncles, make it clear this is a behaviour you are proud of.

Simply showing an interest can often be enough, ask '*How much have you got saved now*?'. Helping them to count the money is a reminder of how well they've done to get this far.

As adults we are often looking only to the future without reflecting on how far we have come. It would help our children if we took a little time every now and then to celebrate reaching our milestones and successes.

3. Bite-sized chunks

If the goal feels overwhelming and out of reach, take a look at ways to break it down into smaller bite-sized chunks.

Setting smaller regular targets, which can be achieved quickly, can help to keep your child interested when the end goal appears out of reach.

For example, teaching a child to ride a bike can be achieved in small steps such as mastering a balance bike, followed by a bike with stabilizers and then a full pedal bike. These small steps are far less daunting and achievable than starting with a full bike.

For savings, this could mean breaking the amount into £5 increments or, if possible, buying their goal in sections, such as different parts of a train track or accessories for a doll.

4. Focus on the feeling

Help them visualise buying or ordering the item, receiving it, unwrapping it, wearing it, playing with it, sharing it and showing it to friends. Find what motivated them to want it, focus on that feeling.

We often want 'things' because of the way they will make us feel, although children don't yet understand this. We may want something because our friends have it, but the feeling is 'belonging' and in part conformity. It's about us sharing and connecting with others.

The best example I can give is children's delight in sticker collections. They've been around for years; I still have my 1986 Panini Football sticker collection. I wasn't the slightest bit interested in football but the idea of collecting and swapping in the playground and being part of something appealed.

My nephew collects Match Attax (the modern day equivalent of my football sticker collection). Initially his parents thought, '*What a waste of money*'. You can spend over £100 trying to get the entire collection and then you can guarantee you'll always have to send off for those last few limited print cards (in addition to the tactic cards, foil cards and rainbow foil cards!).

So, why are sticker book collections still popular in a digital world?

Their continued appeal is down to the way in which children use the stickers (which, let's face it, on their own are hardly exciting):

- How they connect with their peers
- The excitement they feel when they've got a limited edition sticker

- The negotiating and trading in the playground (and the odd fight)
- Pride and a sense of achievement at collecting them all

The major attraction of a sticker book to your child is how it captures the feelings of being a part of something.

Helping your child visualise the feeling of owning the thing they want, playing that drum kit, wearing those latest trainers is the key. It's the feeling that will capture their imagination in the same way that we crave home ownership, holidays or cars.

5. Add an incentive

Depending on the item they are saving for, you may choose to add an incentive (particularly if you intended to buy it anyway). The incentive could be something like:

- If you forego an ice cream, magazine or extra treat this week we'll add the money we would have spent to your savings pot
- If you save the whole amount then we'll buy the 'accessory' to go with it
- If you reach £20 we'll add the final £5
- If you save half, we'll add the other half
- If you reach a different goal (pass your swimming badge, get all of your spellings right), we'll double your current total

> **Tip:** Offer additional pocket money in return for something from them that they wouldn't normally do. For example, vacuuming, reading with their younger sibling etc.

I would urge caution on buying them their goal now in exchange for them paying you back over time, as this often leads to conflict, although this can provide an important lesson in credit. They will soon realise it's no fun paying for a cake you have already eaten.

What if they've changed their goal?

It's fairly likely that as your children go through this journey of goal setting and working towards a goal, whether that's saving money or learning a musical instrument, they are almost guaranteed to lose enthusiasm and change their mind. The goal, which they were incredibly passionate about, is no longer actually exciting at all and has been replaced with something even better.

You have one of two ways to react to this, the first is coercing, persuading and generally cajoling them back into being motivated and excited about their original goal and the second is to accept that through exploring this avenue they have decided that it's not really for them after all.

Definitely don't see this change of heart as failure; in many ways this is great practice for the real world. How many times have we regretted things we have bought? Like purchasing those ill-fitting, high-fashion clothes only to think, 'Why did I think that would suit me?' a month later. It's all part of the learning process.

However, if this change of heart appears to be a very familiar pattern and your child doesn't seem to see anything through, this might be part of a Craver's personality where they believe 'all with be well with the world when I have...'.

If you think your child is jumping from idea to idea, it might be worth encouraging them to see one of their goals through to the end, to feel the satisfaction of compromising how they have spent in order to purchase something they really want.

Step 6: The purchase

I have a romantic image of going to buy your child's longed-for purchase and handing over their piggy bank full of coins to a smiling retailer. However, the reality is probably very different as we tend to make purchases online and pay using cards. As such, I think it is important to plan how you intend to make the purchase.

Deciding on where to make the purchase will depend on a number of factors:

- Availability to purchase instore; some items are only available online, you may not live near a branch of the store you need to buy from
- The age of your child – a younger child who is less likely to have a grasp of real time may find an online order disjointed due to the time they need to wait between purchase and delivery, compared to walking out of a shop with their longed-for new toy
- An older child is much more likely to be online savvy – they will enjoy the process of ordering online and will love the feeling of having a delivery in their name
- Cost; if the item is significantly cheaper online, after taking into account postage, then buying at a high street store might not make financial sense. A bit of research before your child starts saving will help decide which retailer is likely to be the best value
- For services, such as events or concerts, the ticket is likely to be bought in advance of the occasion and most likely online or over the phone

If purchasing at a store I would advocate using cash or a gift card rather than your own credit/debit card. Your child's sense of accomplishment is lost if it is not seen as their money. Convert cash into a gift card so they can physically hand over the gift card and have a sense of ownership of the money.

Tip: *If you do use your card to pay for goods, don't let your child see you enter your PIN for your cards or your online passwords, in case of unexpected transactions. Always ensure you log out of websites and don't allow your card details to be stored, to avoid any unwanted child purchases.*

Comparing offers and discounts at different retailers

A shopping experience can be overwhelming due to the amount of choice available and the constant bombardment of marketing. Discounts and promotions can make a child's purchase more confusing and a less enjoyable experience.

Helping your child to compare offers from different retailers for similar products will help them to decide where to make their purchase.

The following advice is aimed towards older children, who have a better understanding of maths, however younger children can start to understand the principles.

Retailers (and manufacturers) use every marketing trick available to persuade you to spend more; these marketing ploys make it more difficult to compare products and prices. A visit to the supermarket is the ideal opportunity to talk to your child about how to compare offers and make a decision on which one to choose. The promotions are so prominent and there are so many it won't take long before your child has got a handle on most of the tricks to look out for.

The type of price promotions used by supermarkets and other retailers are:

- Buy one get one free
- Buy three for the price of two
- % discount off the original price
- Conditional purchase – buy two for £5 (when normally £3 each), buy one get one half price

In addition to price promotions, retailers and manufacturers will use other ways to encourage us to buy their items, such as:

- % extra free
- 18 for the price of 12
- New and improved versions
- Celebrity endorsements
- Charity donations for each pack sold
- Product placement – putting things together on the shelf to encourage you to buy something which goes with the item you originally planned to buy
- Tokens to save and collect for a toy

We've all bought things because of these offers and ended up throwing away food we haven't eaten or clothes we won't wear. It's only a bargain if you really want and will use the product.

Hesitation

When a child has saved the money themselves, the point of purchase can be a time when they waiver on whether it is still what they want, and this is completely natural. If this money came from the 'Bank of Mum and Dad' there would be no question of whether they wanted the item – of course they do, there are no consequences of not having it.

In comparison, when it's their money they know the resolve it took to save that amount, they know the things they have given up and they know it is their decision on how to spend that money.

> **Tip:** *Savers are much more likely to hesitate when it comes to parting with their hard-saved money. A Craver's overwhelming desire to purchase is likely to overrule any doubts.*

The consumer experience – an awakening

An interesting observation I made when going through this process with one client was how the child had a light bulb moment and realised they had what I can only describe as 'consumer power'.

They suddenly understood that the hard-earned money they had saved in their pocket was very valuable and that they were in complete control of how they spend it.

During a trip to the shop to buy the longed-for item, the child became very aware of other temptations they could spend their money on, from a hot chocolate and muffin, to a new mobile phone cover, to magazines and sweets at the checkout.

Prior to having his own money he had never considered the many ways in which money can be spent. Watching a parent buy items using their card didn't have the same effect because it never seemed real.

The receipt and consumer rights

We want our children to run off and enjoy their new purchase, but for an older child it's worth touching on the purpose of a receipt (or if ordered online, an email confirmation).

Your child might be a bit young to understand that we have consumer rights when we purchase items, but they're not too young to understand that if their beloved item breaks (through no fault of their own), then they'd like it to be replaced.

Under the Sale of Goods Act 1979, consumers have the right to buy goods that are of good quality (fit for purpose), safe and work. We have an expectation that the item we buy does what it was marketed as doing.

Without a proof of purchase (i.e. receipt) you can't return an item to the shop and simply say you bought it there, the shop needs proof.

The receipt will also state how much you paid for an item. If you don't have your receipt and the item is discounted, the retailer will only give you the current price for the goods, which may be less than the amount you paid.

One final purpose of a receipt is to keep a check on what we have bought. With an increase in online banking and payments, keeping track of our spending is getting trickier. We can check our receipts against our bank statements to make sure we haven't been charged twice, that the money has been taken out, and if the money hasn't been taken out yet then we can make sure we have enough money in our accounts to cover it.

The next time your child throws away the receipt with the packaging, it might be worth just reminding them of why they have a receipt.

Tip: *Receipts no longer include your credit card details, but they can contain personal information. Teach your child to guard their personal information carefully from a young age.*

Changing their mind

It's worth touching on the scenario of your child changing their mind and wanting to return the item. There are important things they need to know:

- Each retailer has their own rules on accepting returns, some will not provide refunds unless faulty, others might not give a cash refund, only a voucher or credit note
- Most retailers have a time limit on refunds. The majority are between 14 to 28 days from the date of the receipt (actual days not business days). As a gesture of customer goodwill, some retailers used to give refunds regardless of when the item was bought, however this is now very rare
- Whatever your reason for returning the item you will always need proof of purchase (your receipt)
- There are slightly different rules for some items bought by distance selling (such as telephone or online orders). Distance selling has something called a 'cooling off period'[x] which means the buyer has an amount of time

to review the item and if it's not what they expected they can return it – this is more relevant with services than products

- If returning goods ordered online, they need to look at the retailer's policy on who pays postage to return it, before ordering

For more detailed advice on consumer rights the Citizens Advice Bureau are a good source of information www.adviceguide.org.uk

Step 7: Celebrate, review and repeat

Celebrate your child's achievement with them, tell them you are proud of how well they have done. This is particularly important if your child has saved for a considerable amount of time (anything more than a month in a child's world is officially a long time).

Watch them enjoy their new purchase; if it's a new scooter, share that first ride to the park, if it's a computer game, watch as they set up their character on screen. Sharing their excitement will make your child feel that the effort of saving brings with it huge rewards.

This is the 'reward'. This is them reaching their aim. This is a very important part of the process.

If our children can learn to take time to enjoy and recognise their achievements, before rushing on to the next 'big' thing, they are more likely to find contentment and less likely to be constantly searching for happiness through the next material object.

> *Tip: For younger children it's a good idea to write their name on their new purchase, this might give it a better chance of making its way home if left anywhere.*

For older children/teens, today's social media driven world puts them under increasing pressure to 'share' all that they achieve in life. It might be frustrating to watch friends seemingly having fun whilst they are trying to save money, however it might also have been a motivator to continue saving knowing they can boast about their new purchase online.

From my experience, children who have saved and chosen to use their own money to purchase something are much more likely to look after their new purchase and have a greater sense attachment to it.

I have seen children realise they can use their own money to buy things for others, which brings a different kind of satisfaction and pleasure. This requires sacrifice and compromise on behalf of the child – it's unusual to see this level of comprehension in children under 10 years of age.

Review – was it worth it?

Encourage your child to reflect on decisions they make about money. Reflection is a great way to think differently about decisions we make in the future and to stop us making the same mistakes again.

How did it feel to not spend during the time they were saving? Do they think they made the right choice with what they bought? Was it worth it?

Think of people you know who seem to make bad financial decisions. Do you think they have learned from them or are they likely to make them again? I have friends who have been tempted to buy clothes in the sale because they felt they were getting a bargain, except they were only buying because of the price and the style didn't suit them. Needless to say there are a few items in charity bags with their labels still on – that's when a bargain isn't a bargain.

Managing money is a life skill

Managing money is simply another life skill, like learning to cook, sewing and doing DIY. As with all of these things, regardless of what careers our children pursue, they will be better prepared for life if they can manage their money.

Teaching children how to manage money shouldn't be something that only happens in a classroom. Money is something we deal with every day, so let's get our children involved from a young age, let them be curious, let them make bad decisions on what to buy, mostly let them learn and build healthy attitudes towards managing their money.

Let them experience your decision making (good and bad decisions), let them see where you place your family's priorities when it comes to money.

Perseverance[xi] is one of the greatest gifts we can give our children.

Managing money is an emotional journey

The emotional aspects of money are just as important as the practical. We are often motivated to spend because of how we feel. In the same way as we might eat for comfort, spending can become a habit we use to make ourselves feel better.

A few pointers for you and your child on building a healthy relationship with money:

- Be aware of what motivates you to spend money, if you are easily influenced by others, be careful not to let that impact your finances
- Be honest with yourself, don't make excuses for why you have overspent, just be truthful and accept the position you are now in and take positive action
- Talk and share with people you trust, if you're worried about your money don't keep it to yourself, other people can help you put it into perspective
- If you make financial decisions based on your emotions, don't make the decision immediately, walk away and go back another day

Repeat – what next?

After celebrating reaching their aim, try setting a new one. Try adjusting it based on what they learned about themselves the first time round. Encourage them to set a portion of their money aside to save for something specific and a portion that can be spent 'now'.

As with most of the things our children learn in life, it's often the repetition of experience which brings the greatest learning. Constant reinforcement helps our children to learn when it is safe to cross the road, how to brush their teeth and how to write their own name.

Lifelong learning

Learning to manage your money isn't a one-off event, it requires constant learning in the same way as other life skills.

Most importantly continue to encourage them to take responsibility of their finances and include them in the financial decisions you make.

Closing notes: Your role

Being able to set yourself a financial goal and stick to a budget is the foundation you need for managing your money.

By empowering your child to set aims based around money at a young age, you are helping them to learn what works for them and experience the highs and lows of saving towards something.

You will also be teaching them how to place a value on something they think they want by really understanding the true cost to them, taking into account what they have had to 'give up' to get it.

Whether your child is naturally a Craver or a Saver, your child's most influential teacher in life is you.

Lead by example. You are their constant; your attitudes and guidance will form a significant part of their attitudes and habits.

It is also likely that we will be learning together how to manage our lives and money in this increasingly virtual world. Don't try to have all of the answers, just embrace the questions.

Finally, never give up. This thing called parenthood is a daunting world of highs and lows. By taking one step at a time, we can help them to make sense of the world and learn how to navigate it together.

References

- '*Emotional Intelligence – why it can matter more than IQ*', Daniel Goleman, 1996, ISBN 0 7475 2830 6
- '*The secret of happy children*', Steve Biddulph, 1994, ISBN 0 7225 3669 0
- '*The power of habit; Why we do what we do and how to change*', Charles Duhigg, 2013, ISBN 9781847946249
- '*Their name is today; reclaiming childhood in a hostile world*', Johann Christoph Arnold, 2014, ISBN 9780874866124
- '*Rich dad, Poor dad*' Robert T. Kiyosaki, 2011, ISBN 9781612680002
- '*Willpower*' Roy F. Baumeister and John Tierney, 2011. ISBN 978014104948-9

Websites

www.pfeg.org.uk (Personal Finance Education Group
www.themoneycharity.co.uk
www.themoneyadviceservice.co.uk
www.uswitch.com
www.gohenry.co.uk
www.ukcardsassociation.org.uk
www.roosterbank.com
www.qwiddle.com
www.moneysupermarket.com
www.moneyville.com
www.nsandi.com
www.gov.uk
www.adviceguide.org.uk

About the author

To most people, money isn't a particularly exciting thing to be passionate about, but to me, your perspective on money is truly captivating.

Let me tell you more. For me, the captivating thing is how money gives us freedom in life, freedom to make choices, take opportunities and realise our dreams. I'm not talking about lottery wins or high salaries; I'm simply talking about making the most of what we have. Focusing on what it is we want and achieving it.

This passion came from my parents, who made the most of every penny.

The pre 'Look after your pennies' years

Armed with an interest in money, the obvious career path for me was a degree in Business Studies followed by a 17-year career in financial services, gaining a Masters in Business Administration from Warwick University Business School along the way.

I will be forever grateful for the experiences I had and the character-defining challenges I faced while working for global companies. I now feel it's time to pay back some of that learning.

Personal life

I was born and raised in Birmingham and now live in Warwickshire with my husband and two young sons.

After the birth of my second son, I decided to take a career break to concentrate on motherhood and exploring whether I could make a business from my idea of financial mentoring.

I greatly appreciate the time you have taken to read my work. Please consider leaving a review wherever you bought the book or telling your friends about it.

If you would like to find out more about what I do, my social media links are below or you can contact me at:

Email: fay@lookafteryourpennies.com

Website: www.lookafteryourpennies.com

Facebook: www.facebook.com/yourpennies

Twitter: @yourpennies

End Notes

---

[i] For more information on the theory behind Instant Gratification, read *'The Marshmallow Test – Understanding self-control and how to master it'* by Walter Mischel

[ii] Source: www.uswitch.com, comparison website

[iii] Source: www.theukcardsassociation.org.uk, information correct as at December 2014

[iv] A contactless transaction is when a payment card is placed near the payment device for the amount to be taken from the account. The card doesn't need to be swiped into the card machine or a PIN entered. Mostly for transactions under £25.

[v] Source: The Financial Conduct Authority www.fca.org.uk

[vi] Source: *'Emotional Intelligence'* – Daniel Goleman (page 62)

[vii] Information taken from company websites, correct as at December 2014

[viii] Individual Savings Accounts – these are tax-free savings for a certain amount of money each year (in 2014/2015 tax year this is £4,000). Source: www.gov.uk

[ix] Premium Bonds are operated by National Savings and Investments. Rather than earning interest, each bond is entered into a monthly prize draw to win tax-free cash. Source: www.nsandi.com

[x] Source: Citizens advice www.adviceguide.org.uk, Check for details of specific details

[xi] Source: Emotional Intelligence – Daniel Goleman

Printed in Great Britain
by Amazon.co.uk, Ltd.,
Marston Gate.